A HUNGRY
HILL TRINITY

Life and Times of Three Generations

JOAN MORRIS REILLY

To: Grandpa, Mom, Dad & Michael

May we meet at the crossroads...

TABLE OF CONTENTS

ACKNOWLEDGEMENTS

This collection of memories was inspired by three people who have all passed on; my grandfather, Jim Cabey, my mother, Rita Cabey Morris and a cousin, Andrew Donnellan. Like most Hungry Hill residents, they were people of faith who thrived on simple philosophies--life wasn't always easy but it was more or less fair and, if you worked hard and took care of your family, you'd be okay.

My relatives were very private people. MYOB was a mantra that was passed on and is still alive and well today. They were also very humble people and never "broke their arm patting themselves on the back." Despite their personal reticence and reserve, however, they and others in the family were natural storytellers who preserved their place in time by passing down stories from their lives to the next generations who picked up the thread and kept this hands-on history going. They shared their lives gladly and often and told us things "unknown to kings" about family and about life. My generation added our own unique experiences to this labor of love.

I appreciate the support of my children, Jim and Beth, and my siblings. Special thanks to my sister Cheryl for her graphic design knowledge and to my niece, Amy B. Perrault, for the outstanding cover design, and to my brothers--Dick, for his crystal clear memory of facts and figures, Mark, for his enthusiasm and knack of finding the right word and, my late brother, Michael, for his youthful "joie de vivre."

I am grateful for the recall of numerous people, and for my cousin Patricia Reardon's ongoing research and interest in our roots. I will forever be indebted to the former *Hungry Hill* magazine, for publishing my first attempts at writing about my memories. They were also a valuable reference for other stories. Also, the local history room at the Connecticut Valley Historical Museum offered a wealth of information on the history of Springfield.

Joan Morris Reilly

PREFACE

Hungry Hill—an area of Springfield, Massachusetts with indefinite boundaries, located between Mercy Hospital on lower Carew Street near the north end of the city and the area around Liberty School on the other end. One end of Hungry Hill was city living and differed from the upper Carew Street end where I grew up, which was like living in the country. There are many stories of how Hungry Hill got its name. The most popular one is that it was named by cops on the beat as there were no restaurants in the area. Whatever the source of the name, it represents the bastion of all that was and is Irish in Springfield.

My grandfather's generation, the immigrants, mostly Irish, but not exclusively, settled on Hungry Hill in the early 1900s. They set the tone and laid the foundation for my mother's generation who lived out their lives against a backdrop of major world events and were, subsequently, known as the "Greatest Generation" and, finally there was my generation, who were the last to know the uniqueness of the area and the first to experience the dramatic changes.

The Hungry Hill of my generation was our own version of Camelot, gone forever. It lives only in the memories of those of us who shared the sights, sounds and smells of an idyllic childhood as we passed through this coherent, safe place. A kid's imagination ruled in these familiar comfortable surroundings where no one ever locked doors.

The neighborhood, then, was a melting pot of ethnic backgrounds. There were Irish families; (at one point, Cabey family members lived in five houses on Laurence Street, a compound of sorts). There were also Greek families, Italian, Swedish, Polish, Scottish, French, several Yankee Protestants and others. We co-existed peacefully in this pastoral setting of dirt roads, woods, vegetable gardens, fruit trees, dogs, cats, chickens, ducks, an enormous goose named Friday and goats grazing in the goat fields at the end of Laurence Street.

There were comforting daily sounds like a rooster crowing every morning, the whistle at the Westinghouse plant announcing the start of shifts and loud planes heading for Westover Air Force Base in Chicopee. I can close my eyes and still hear kids being called home for supper simultaneously at four or five different houses. After supper, the melodic sound of kids' laughter and a lone voice yelling "olly olly infree" were common occurrences as a tin can placed in the middle of the road was kicked in the air during summertime rituals of hide and seek.

Everything we needed was within walking distance-- schools, churches, playgrounds, a library, a movie theater, three doctors' offices located in their homes, several markets and grocery stores, drug stores with soda fountains, two hospitals nearby and easy access to public transportation for anything else.

In addition, there was a cadre of home delivery men; milkmen, the Hathaway Bakery man (Louie the Baker), a ragman that bought old clothing, shoes and almost anything else one wanted to sell (one sister, as a toddler, sold her baby bottle to him for 25 cents) and, the John Hancock Life Insurance man, Mr. O'Brien (Obie), a charming, dapper man who made weekly collections for the premiums due on small life insurance policies.

No one had any money but, in so many important ways we were not poor. We may have lacked an abundance of material possessions, but, we reaped the benefits of a positive lifestyle with sturdy, unbending standards to live by; secure in the knowledge that we were loved and valued. This was reinforced on a daily basis by parents, grandparents and teachers who had more faith in us than we ever had in ourselves.

The reality of life, of course, is change. While Hungry Hill still exists geographically, it is not the "holy ground" of my grandfather's time and bears little resemblance to my era. The generations in this book experienced a life that was certainly not without certain hardships. However, not in their wildest dreams could they have imagined living with drug-related crimes and violence, the lack of social mores and the breakdown of family structure that is present in today's more predatory world.

THE EARLY YEARS

THE EARLY YEARS AT A GLANCE

Hungry Hill became an official neighborhood between 1900 and 1930.

Cottages were moved from the Advent Christian Campgrounds on Stockman and Hastings Streets and Phoenix Terrace to the Lennox Platte in the fringe area of Hungry Hill. This area consisted of Border, Laurence and Wilson Streets. and was all woods with a spring and a brook that emptied into Hogan's Pond. Cellar holes were hand dug for these cottages.

Traffic consisted of horsedrawn wagons for the garbage collector and the ragman and, residents running out with a shovel to get the droppings. They were way ahead of their time; they knew the value of organic fertilizer and this saved a trip to Carey's cow flop to get "meadow muffins."

In the winter, trolley cars were equipped with a snowplow shooting snow high into the air on both sides of the track and gangs of boys would hang on to the sides and backs of the trolley for a free ride.

The old Boston & Albany railroad steamers belched out black smoke and colored the wash on the clotheslines near the tracks.

Working at the Westinghouse was a way of life for many Hungry Hill and East Springfield residents for 50 years.

Wakes were held in homes before funeral homes came into being—neighbors would collect money and buy flowers.

Coal was delivered by a chute in the cellar window and everyone had their turn at "banking" the furnace at night.

Feeding a quarter to the meter was a regular occurrence so the kitchen stove wouldn't run out of gas or if you had a kerosene stove, making sure the big glass jug was filled with kerosene.

Winter clothing always included long johns or union suits with trap doors which stood alone when brought in frozen from the clothesline.

Miss Abbey could be seen in her horse and buggy going to work at Armory Street School where she was principal.

A sign of the times

Thomas Cabey   Andrew Cabey

James Cabey

Kitchen racket crowd at Carey's--1920s

Marie, Jim
and Rita Cabey
Circa 1918

Sunday mornings at Andy Cabey's--1920s

21

HUNGRY HILL PIONEERS
Some of the First Settlers on the Hill

The Cabey Family immigrated to this country from Kilmaley, County Clare, Ireland in the early 1900's. James, Andrew and Thomas Cabey lived with their sister, Mary Ellen (Minnie) Cabey Donnellan who lived on Lillian Street before they settled on Hungry Hill; James and Andrew on Laurence Street and Thomas on Wilbur Street. Another brother, Patrick who had come over earlier, died of typhoid fever shortly after his arrival.

The Cabey brothers settled into their new country in their Hungry Hill enclave, worked hard and raised families. They socialized with relatives and friends from the old country. Along with the Dillons, the Donnellans, the Careys, Pat Leahy, Martin Wynne, P.J. Hiney and others, they kept their ties to Ireland strong by membership in the Ancient Order of Hibernians, Council 22 and were founding members of the John Boyle O'Reilly Club. They were among the first members of Our Lady of Hope Church and its Holy Name Society.

Many of their descendants still reside on Hungry Hill. Their immigrant eyes would have been pleased to see upwards of 90 descendants at a family reunion held in 1998 at the John Boyle O'Reilly Club.

Another family reunion was held in County Clare, Ireland, in September 2008. Close to 100 people attended including 25 from the United States.

GRACE AND GRIT
Aggie Frawley's Precarious Journey

Agnes Frawley Cabey was born in Shean, Kilmaley, County Clare, Ireland; the youngest child of Daniel and Bridget Frawley. When Aggie was four years old, her mother died and she was sent to live with her aunt and uncle, Anne & John Frawley, two fields over. She stayed with them for three years in Ireland and when they decided to leave for America, her father was still not able to care for her. He made arrangements for her to live with his sisters in Lowell, Massachusetts. Aggie accompanied Anne & John and their children on this journey to a new unknown life in another country.

Try to imagine a child of seven years old who had lived with one set of relatives and was now leaving the only home she ever knew to go across the ocean with them to live with other relatives she had never met. She had a large name tag pinned to her coat for identification. Conditions in steerage were horrific and her two cousins, Jane and Bridget died of ship fever. Only her aunt and uncle and she and her cousin Patrick managed to survive the trip.

Aggie lived in Lowell for 10 or 12 years. When she was 18 or so, she returned to Ireland and stayed with her father, brother and sister for a brief period. Times were very hard and in 1904, she left once again for America to stay with her aunts in Lowell.

At a wedding reception there she met Jim Cabey, a young man from the same parish in Ireland, who lived on Hungry Hill in Springfield, MA. Like the Irish song that proclaims, "going to a wedding is the makings of another," a courtship began.

They were married in Lowell in 1909. They took the train to Springfield for their wedding reception and began their new life on Hungry Hill. Their home was an Adventist campground house that was moved from around Phoenix Terrace and Wilbur Street to a newly developed plot on Laurence Street. There, Jim and Agnes had four children, Marie, James, Rita and William.

Aggie was a truly beautiful woman with delicate features. Her photos depict her as a classic Gibson Girl. She had a very quick temper which was balanced by the quiet, easy going nature of her husband Jim. She was a devoted mother and wife and was known as "Auntie Addie" to various nieces and nephews. Her oldest child, Marie, recalls their mother taking them for walks, watching the construction of Liberty School and going to the daisy fields which were located where Van Sickle Junior High now stands.

Sadly, Aggie died of Bright's Disease, an inflammation of the kidneys, a few weeks after her son, Billy was born in 1922, leaving Jim with a newborn and three other children ages 8, 9 and 11 years old, to raise by himself. Rita Cabey vividly recalled her mother's wake, which was held in their home for three days.

For awhile, Jim hired housekeepers to help with the children, the cooking and the housework. This was a very difficult period as some of the housekeepers were not the best people. One of them was let go for stealing Aggie's Irish linens. Another confiscated the food meant for the children and gave them "prune juice sandwiches" for a meal. As they got older, Marie and Rita assumed the housekeeping duties and the meal preparation.

Jim never married again. He, like many in that era, believed that there was only one love in a lifetime. He wouldn't dream of getting married for convenience, just to have someone take care of the children and keep the house, even though it was very much needed.

Jim lived to see many grandchildren. He always kept his wedding picture on the wall in his home so his grandkids would be aware of this beautiful woman, their grandmother, who, despite the adversity of her early years or maybe because of it, dedicated the rest of her short life to her husband and children.

THE EARLY YEARS

SOCIALIZING IN THE EARLY YEARS
Now Those Voices All are Silent, Gone Before Us...

Part of the entertainment at Irish family gatherings and "kitchen rackets" in the 1920's included someone giving recitations. Annie Dillon McGuane was a cousin of the Cabeys. She was a talented, flamboyant lady who could recite Irish poetry and readings from memory. She was truly a woman ahead of her time who possessed a powerful voice and a flair for dramatics which mesmerized her audience and took them to another place and time.

These are excerpts of recitations that she acted out using gestures and voice projection as recalled by Rita Cabey Morris and Andrew Donnellan. She usually began by saying, "Let me sit down a moment, I have a stone in my shoe."

Down in Lehigh Valley
Anonymous

Let me sit down a minute, stranger,
Yes, I'm a tramp, what of it?
I ain't done a thing to you
Some folks think we're no good;
You needn't start your swearin
But a tramp has to live, I reckon,
A stone got in my shoe though
they say we never should...

Bold Robert Emmet
Tom Maguire

Bold Robert Emmet, the darling of Erin
Bold Robert Emmet will die with a smile
Farewell companions both loyal and daring,
I'll lay down my life for the Emerald Isle...

Willy Reilly
Anonymous

"Oh! Rise Up, Willy Reilly,
and come along with me,
I mean for to go with you and leave this counterie
To leave my father's dwelling,
his houses and free land,"
And away goes Willy Reilly
and his dear Coolen Ban...

Dawn on the Irish Coast
John Locke

Glory to God, but there it is –
The dawn on the hills of Ireland!
God's angels lifting the night's black veil
From the fair, sweet face of my sireland!
O Ireland! Isn't it grand you look –
Like a bride in her rich adorning!
With all the pent-up love of my heart,
I bid you the top of the morning!

Coach the Piper
John Keegan

One winters' day long, long ago,
When I was a little fellow,
A piper wandered to our door,
Grey-headed, blind, and yellow
And, oh! How glad was my young heart,
Though earth and sky looked dreary,
To see the stranger and his dog—
Poor "Pinch" and Coach O'Leary ...

The Early Years

Kitchen Rackets on Hungry Hill
By Rita Cabey Morris as told to Joan Morris Reilly

Weekends were a reprieve from classes at the High School of Commerce. Most Saturdays in those days, I looked forward to the weekly serials at the Cleveland Street Movie Theater, which was actually a converted garage. For the price of a dime, we were treated to the latest adventures of Tom Mix and other silent screen heroes dramatically accompanied by a piano player. And, if you sat in the lucky seat, you won a prize – talk about fun!

This Saturday, however, was different as it was the Columbus Day weekend and our friend Pat Carey had killed a pig. This ritual was always followed by a "kitchen racket" a weekend gathering held several times a year. This time, the kitchen racket was at our house, so, I had a lot of cleaning to do. Since my mother died several years before, my sister Marie and I were in charge of the housework and the care of Billy, the youngest in our family. My father Jim Cabey was busy preparing the home brew for this shindig.

During Prohibition and long after its repeal, nearly every Irish immigrant family in the area had a still in the cellar where they brewed their own beer. Dadda and the other men made beer using malt and hops and sometimes on special occasions, they made something stronger known as "scomption" or "the recipe."

The kitchen rackets were a welcome break from our routine and a chance to see people like the Ryans and the Kanaveys a large, robust band of Carey relatives from Mineola, New York who loved coming to the "country."

In addition, there were the regulars from Hungry Hill like

Pat Leahy, P.J. Hiney, Martin Wynn and Uncle Tom Cabey, along with their families and other kindred spirits. There was always top-notch entertainment at these parties. Uncle Johnny Donnellan brought his fiddle. Auntie Mary Cabey and Uncle Mike Donnellan played the concertina. Morris Devine played the accordion and Uncle Andrew Cabey was a wonderful step dancer. Others like Annie Dillon, gave recitations.

The dancing went on all night--the jigs, reels, half sets, Stack of Barley Reels and Verse of Viennas never stopped until it was time to go to 6 o'clock mass at our Lady of Hope Church the next morning.

I distinctly recall one particular time at Uncle Andrew's house when the vibrations from the dancing dislodged the chimney pipe from the wood stove and no one even noticed until the room started to fill up with smoke!

After Mass and some sleep, we would regroup on Sunday afternoons usually at the Carey's house on Hamlet Street, for the last few hours of this grand reunion.

These long ago memories of good friends and good times will stay with me always. I can still hear each guest as they came into our house, calling out the same cheerful greeting, sometimes in Gaelic "God Bless All Here" and, you know, he truly did!

SUNDAY MORNINGS FOR THE CRAIC

*Craic: Irish word for talk and banter of good company;
getting together to have a laugh and take a break from
being serious about life.*

From the late 1920s or thereabouts, Sunday mass at Our
Lady of Hope Church was usually followed by a gathering
of men in Uncle Andrew's kitchen on Laurence Street. Jim
Cabey, Tom Cabey, Uncle Mike Donnellan, Uncle Johnny
Donnellan, Pat Leahy, Martin Wynne, Mr. Devine and others
would place their chairs in a semi-circle and have cigars,
beer, and shots of the "recipe" made in the cellar, as well as
food provided by Auntie Mary Cabey.

There were several accomplished musicians in the group
so there was often Irish music added to the mix.   Mostly,
they loved to talk about anything that was going on in their
lives and the world at these infamous forums. This tradition
was ongoing for many years. As some of the older members
of the group passed on, Bud Cabey continued to have
gatherings at his home into the 1960s with more music added
to the craic.

Bud's later sessions included popular accordion players
such as Joey Derrane and Donnie McCarthy, who comple-
mented fiddle players like Harold Meara and Uncle Johnny
Donnellan and the amazing concertinas of Uncle Mike
Donnellan and Auntie Mary Cabey. Bud joined in on the
accordion or the piano at these original jam sessions. As kids
in the 1950s, we were always welcomed there for a visit and
to show them our latest Irish step dancing or whatever else
we had going on.

How great it would have been to have had today's recording
technology to preserve some of those priceless moments in
time that live only in the memories of a very few.

LAST STOP – BOTTLE PARK
Liberty Street's Own "Toonerville" Trolley

Public transportation in the first quarter of the 20th century, before busses, consisted of trolley cars which ran on metal tracks in the center of the street and collected electric current from an overhead cable strung above the tracks.

For many years, the last trolley car to Hungry Hill left downtown Springfield at around midnight and went as far as what is now known as Bottle Park. The trolley tracks were embedded in most of Liberty Street but stopped at Carew Street. Eventually tracks were added to Carew Street to encourage development of the outer areas. But at one time, anyone who lived beyond Carew and Liberty had to walk the rest of the way home.

In warm weather, open cars were used and the cool breeze was welcomed on a hot night. Each car held about 25 to 30 passengers and there was a conductor who collected the ten cent fare, made change from a coin collector on his belt and issued transfers when they were requested. A Mom & Pop store, where the Liberty Package Store is now located would stay open late for the trolley customers to enjoy a soda or ice cream before they started their trek up Carew Street.

It's hard to imagine how limited your options were for getting anywhere in those days. School transportation didn't exist and it was not unusual to walk several miles to attend an event or go to work or school.

WESTINGHOUSE –
Employer and Neighbor

The Westinghouse was located in East Springfield, a few minutes from Hungry Hill. During peak years, almost half of the workforce lived in the area. Hungry Hill and East Springfield residents didn't need clocks during the Westinghouse years. The familiar whistle moaned at the beginning of each shift – 6:00 a.m., 2:00 p.m. and 10:00 p.m. The last stop for the Carew to East Springfield bus was, until the 1970s located in front of the Westinghouse plant. The Westinghouse era was an outstanding example of business and residents living and growing together with reciprocal benefits to the community.

Westinghouse was organized in Springfield in 1915 as a firearms manufacturer because of the reputation of Springfield craftsmen for precision workmanship. In the beginning, they made rifles for the Czar of Russia and following our country's entry into World War I, they manufactured and delivered the first two Browning machine guns in time to sail to France with General Pershing.

At the end of World War I, the manufacture of firearms was discontinued and for more than a year, the factory was closed. The plant was reopened in 1919 for the manufacture of automotive equipment and small motors and in 1921, commercial radio apparatus. Gradually, the manufacture of motors assumed major importance and new lines of products which required motors were added, the first being the Westinghouse fan line.

Again, to take advantage of the skill and reliability of Springfield craftsmen, the machines and tools for making electric fans were transferred from Newark, N.J.

to Springfield making this plant one of the largest producing centers in the country for fans of all types and sizes. Automotive equipment manufacturing was terminated in 1926 to accommodate the growth of the small motor business.

In 1929, Westinghouse added refrigeration units to its variety of products. The cold making mechanism for domestic refrigerator units quickly became the major product of the East Springfield plant and remained so until World War II. Other lines added during this period were coolers for Coca Cola, food mixers, room heaters, air conditioning units, vacuum cleaners, water coolers and milk coolers.

In 1940, Westinghouse volunteered to make weapons again for the allies in World War II. A few weeks after the attack on Pearl Harbor, Westinghouse production facilities were devoted 100 percent to making weapons for war or war-related products, i.e., bomb fuses, fire control equipment, radio and radar apparatus, tank gun stabilizers, special parts for torpedoes and many other precision products which required painstaking craftsmanship.

The radio products division produced radio transmitters for planes and ships requiring more than 200 parts each. The conversion from peacetime production to manufacturing exclusively for war purposes took less than five months. The number of employees increased from 2561 in January 1942 to 5300 in July of 1944. About 25 percent of these workers were women. Westinghouse workers were given the Army-Navy "E" Award for their rapid conversion and excellence of war production. This award was continuously renewed every six months during the war.

During the war years, rallies were held to keep workers

aware of the importance of meeting schedules in producing materials for the fighting forces. In 1943, Lowell Thomas was master of ceremonies at a rally at the East Springfield plant. Other rallies had the governor of Massachusetts as a speaker and a crew member who helped bomb Tokyo. Contests were held for slogans like "Produce and Win" and "Make it Good." At the conclusion of World War II, it was back to peacetime operations and a massive expansion program.

Springfield was among the first cities in the country to have a radio station due to the location of the Westinghouse plant. Radiophone station WBZ began broadcasting from the Westinghouse on September 19, 1921, with coverage of opening day of the Eastern States Exposition, now the Big E in West Springfield. One of the first commercial license in the country was issued to WBZ by the Department of Commerce during President Harding's term for the purpose of broadcasting speech and entertainment. The first World Series baseball game was broadcast on October 10, 1923 between the New York Yankees and the New York Giants.

In 1924, WBZA, a "booster" transmitter that improved reception in the Boston area went on the air. Numerous radio "firsts" are credited to this station – the first broadcast of a major league hockey game between the Boston Bruins and the Montreal Canadians on December 1, 1924; the first broadcast of a Harvard football game, the first broadcast of a Boston Symphony concert, followed by a Boston Pops concert the next year. This station was the first to use a remote van for on-the-scene reporting of news.

In 1927, WBZ moved from the Westinghouse plant to the Hotel Kimball in downtown Springfield and WBZA-Boston conducted the first synchronization tests in the country—

broadcasting from one studio for reception on both stations. Two years later, the now synchronized WBZ-WBZA upped its power to 50,000 watts, moved the programming center from Springfield to Boston and switched the call letters of the two stations.   In 1962, Westinghouse announced that it was discontinuing operation of WBZA in Springfield so they could acquire another station in New York. The call letters have remained famous and WBZ continues to broadcast from Boston with a 50,000 watt channel that reaches up and down the East Coast. But, it all started right here, in East Springfield, in the shadow of Hungry Hill.

In 1950, the Westinghouse plant had 18 buildings and the finest machines and tools available. The work force totaled 4600 men and women from all racial, national and religious backgrounds. The workers were represented by three unions and were considered to be pioneers in the area of labor and management sitting down to solve common problems. In addition to the plant, there were sales and service organizations in Springfield serving industrial and central station customers throughout Western Mass. Also, the Westinghouse Electric Supply Company served as a national distributor which warehoused electrical, industrial and outdoor equipment and home appliances.

Such was life until the occurrence of a major strike at the plant in 1956 idled most of the work force and set the stage for a decade or more of turbulent changes. Who could have predicted that a way of life was coming to an end? These people had survived a Depression and a world war and had good jobs with a successful company. The future looked bright and promising – after all, "you can be sure if it's Westinghouse"…can't you?

In 1958, rumors were rampant that the East Springfield

operations were going to be transferred to Ohio. From a survey conducted at Westinghouse plants across the country, it was concluded that the Company would be better off from an economic standpoint to transfer manufacturing to the Mansfield and Columbus, Ohio plants. Some of the explanations for this proposed action were a better tax break and a union more docile in its wage demands which meant a lot in the overall marketing picture.

The February 27, 1959 issue of the *Springfield Daily News* confirmed the worst fears of the workforce at Westinghouse —"1400 to be Laid Off at Westinghouse." This was the pattern for the next decade until, finally, in December of 1970, the last 200 employees were laid off and the East Springfield plant closed its doors forever.

Westinghouse today is a myriad of consolidations, mergers and numerous divisions with unfamiliar names— far from the household word that it once was and for most area residents, it's just a memory of a way of life in another time.

THE GREATEST GENERATION

The Greatest Generation

The Greatest Generation at a Glance

Summers at Hogan's Pond with planes overhead from the Springfield Airport.

Playing agates or marbles and having the dirty knuckles to prove it, bending birch trees down in the woods and catapulting smaller kids high into the air.

Family picnics at Van Horn Park – potatoes cooked in the fire and hot dogs on a stick. Crossing the rickety suspension bridge over the frog pond and then getting wet in the newly opened paddle pool.

Street roller skating with keys or going to the Victory Roller Rink on the corner of Carew and Newbury Street. Winters tobogganing or sliding down the sand banks at the end of Pembroke Street on a piece of sheet metal or an old dishpan.

Ice skating at the old Lombard reservoir near the current Kendall Commons Nursing Home or at Carey's cow flop or walking to Van Horn Park to skate and watching Father Sexton and Father Martin have races across the pond.

Doctors made house calls for $5.00. An office visit was $2.00. (Note, this was the total cost, not a co-pay).

Cashing in empty soda or beer bottles at Goldberg's (Carew Pharmacy) and using the money to buy a double dip ice cream cone at the Igloo two doors down or for admission to the Liberty Theater especially on dish night.

Party line phones – five or six homes sharing one line.

Running very fast by the railroad tracks because of the hobo camp or "Hooverville" located there and seeing Hockitty Graves in a 3-piece suit selling apples he collected on his daily walk.

Young men joining the Civilian Conservation Corporation (CCC) during the Great Depression as there were no jobs, nationwide.

Al Smith ran for President—the first Catholic to do so. Someone painted his name on Parkside Street and it didn't fade for a very long time.

The card with big numbers that was put in the window to let the Liberty Ice and Fuel man know how big a piece of ice to leave —10 cents, 15 cents, 20 cents or 25 cents worth.

Food rationing and stamps issued by the government. Businesses with the Blue Eagle NRA sticker in their window.

A red and blue banner with a gold star in a window signifying that a family member was killed in World War II.

Bud Cabey chilling a batch of
home brew from the "White House"

Cabey social gatherings -- 1930's

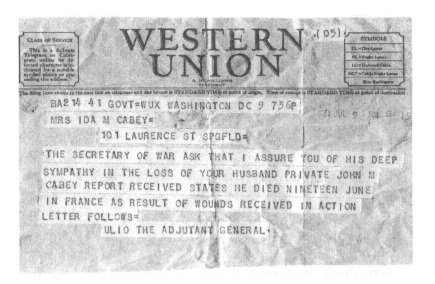

The price of war

John Michael Cabey
1914-1944

Johnny, we hardly knew you!

WHITE HOUSE YEARS
Prohibition Ways and Means
By Rita Cabey Morris as told to Joan Morris Reilly

Hardly a day goes by that the White House isn't mentioned in the media. Most people immediately think of Washington, D.C., the President, etc. When I hear those words, however, I have fond memories of something a lot closer to home.

During the era of Prohibition and long after its repeal, many households produced their own alcoholic beverages. My Irish immigrant family in the Hungry Hill section of Springfield, Massachusetts, had a still in the cellar which we referred to among ourselves as "the White House." This was basically a whitewashed wooden cupboard which contained the supplies and implements needed to make beer using malt and hops. Sometimes, on special occasions, something stronger, known as "the recipe" or "scomption," was concocted. To this day, I'm not sure if referring to the White House was the Irish way of tweaking the federal government for this unpopular legislation or that it simply described the white cupboard that held their answer to Prohibition.

An amusing story passed down in the family was that of a cousin whose father was employed at the Springfield Armory. He told of their still being assembled in various departments of the Armory and then delivered in a government truck to his house! He added that when they got the still working, they needed something to strain the ingredients so they used his mother's lace curtain which turned purple. This gave a whole new meaning to "lace curtain Irish."

Folklore or not, the white houses provided the spirits for my family's social gatherings of that era. Kitchen rackets were weekend gatherings of friends and relatives held several times a year with music, dancing, good hearty food, (often, a pig was butchered) and, of course, the latest batch of home brew.

Prohibition, kitchen rackets and most of the people that attended are just memories now. As for white houses, the last operating one in the family was dismantled in the 1960s following the death of the cousin who had kept the tradition going.

One granddaughter, raised in that house, had an interesting experience at Liberty School around 1950 when the teacher asked the class if anyone knew where the White House was located. Patricia raised her hand and answered proudly, "It's in my grandfather's cellar!" She became very upset and cried when everyone laughed at her answer and the teacher told her she was mistaken.

This same girl grew up and married an agent of the Alcohol, Tobacco and Firearms Bureau, who had some anxious moments when Bud Cabey toasted their engagement with the latest batch of the "recipe" from the last existing white house in the family!

HOGAN'S POND IN THE DEPRESSION YEARS
By Rita Cabey Morris as told to Joan Morris Reilly

Hogan's Pond was a great place to swim in the late 20s and 30s. These were years when no one had any money to go very far. As teenagers during these years, by necessity, we found enjoyment in simple pursuits that didn't cost anything. Wonderful friendships and camaraderie flourished as we were all in the same boat economically. Groups of Hungry Hill guys and gals would walk to Hogan's from the end of Strong Street, through the fields across the log over the little stream to the pond.

Despite some mysterious ear infections and stern warnings from Dr. Greaney, we frequented Hogan's on a regular basis to swim and hang out. The Careys, the Wescotts, the Cabeys, including myself, Ida Caron and numerous others whiled away many summer days at the pond behind the ice house where we swam, sometimes until very late at night.

One particular day always comes to mind when I think about summers at Hogan's Pond. It was a warm Sunday afternoon when Ida Caron, Mary Wescott, Ernie Clowes and myself took a walk and naturally gravitated to our favorite hangout—Hogan's. We didn't go in the pond that day but we were exploring some of the surrounding area just walking and talking. Ida was wearing a new pink dress and was feeling really good about herself as she walked ahead of us with Ernie Clowes. Suddenly, she let out a scream as she sank into a hole before our eyes! Our first reaction was to laugh, thinking she fell into a mud puddle.

When we realized she was struggling and couldn't get out, it dawned on us that this was quicksand and she was sinking! Ernie managed to pull her out by the arms, while Mary and

I cheered him on. What a sight they were! The new pink dress was ripped to the waist and covered with mud. Ernie was covered with mud also and pretty well shook up.

As we made our way home, the realization of this close call really made our adrenaline flow. But, this harrowing experience didn't stop us from going to Hogan's again and again. Hogan's was as familiar as our backyards. We never equated it with anything but a comfort zone.

Ernie became the original "Hogan's Hero" as we told and retold this story. Also, we were now the experts on the terrain as we could point out where this pocket of quicksand was located, which was pretty much off the beaten track.

Fortunately, we never did hear about anyone else finding it the hard way!

CCC CAMP – SIGN OF THE TIMES
From a CCC Camp in Goshen, New Hampshire
Reprinted Letter from Jimmie Cabey to his sister

November 16, 1933

Hello Rita,

I received your letter and was glad to hear from you. Boy, it's cold as hell up here now and we got plenty of snow. This is wild country. We are up on a mountain; the place is six miles from NewPort and 125 miles from home. We took a train, then a bus to get here. In June when we got here, we had to put up our tents and the mess tent which was a lot of work. There's 228 men in our gang.

My cold is getting better, thanks for the cough syrup. It's hard work up here but I've gained 3 pounds and I feel good. Thanks for the buck, Rita. I'm sending a Happy Days Paper. Never mind sending the newspaper, we get them up here but would you send some stamps when you write.

Gee, I'm glad Dad got a suit, he needed one bad enough. Is Dad working steady? I'll bet they had a hell of a time over the cow.

We have a new little cat up here. He is white and he looks like a snowball How's Bill and Marie? Why don't Marie drop a line once in awhile or is she too busy? Armistice Day didn't mean much to us up here.

Gee, it's nice and warm in the barracks, we got three stoves in them. But, we have to get up at 5:30 now. That's not so good, it's pitch dark. They're getting strict as hell now too but the grub is good so everything is good.

Well, I guess that's about all. So long, see you soon.
Give my love to all.
Jimmie

The Greatest Generation

Friends from the Greatest Generation
By Rita Cabey Morris as told to Joan Morris Reilly

For several years, there was a popular TV show called "Friends" which is basically about a group of young men and women who are there for each other. The show was such a big hit that it resulted in several spinoffs of this same theme, as if friends were a rare phenomenon.

I'm from a different era and I, among others, can give those fictional TV friends a run for their money with real-life friendships, minus the whining and bed-hopping portrayed weekly on TV.

I grew up in the Hungry Hill section of Springfield, Massachusetts, during the 1920s and 30s and was part of a large group of friends, both male and female. Our friends included myself, Ida Caron, Mary Wescott, Bud and John Cabey, Frank Carey, Helen Carey, Mario Vigiliano, Joe Vigiliano, Gino Serra, Eddie Sharon, Florence Ethier and other assorted siblings and chums. We learned about life against a backdrop of major world events.

As kids, we helped to make home brew during Prohibition. As teenagers we "hung out" together; dated each other, spent hours doing marathon dancing, swam at Hogan's Pond and expanded our circle of friends. Young people will be surprised to know that camping wasn't invented in the 80s or 90s. As far back as 1925, we went camping in Enfield, Massachusetts, one of the towns now under the Quabbin Reservoir.

During the Great Depression, some of us managed to finish high school. Most worked hard at various jobs for a few dollars a week to help our families put food on the table and many of our male friends entered CCC camps. Depression years were a time of shortages and sacrifices but one thing that was never in short supply was spirit. We, along with the rest of the country, learned to pull together to find creative solutions to shortages and help one another.

During the war years, we worked in wartime production factories, used ration stamps and covered our windows during "blackout periods." Another friend, Joe Conway, was the civil defense warden in the area and he demanded strict adherence to the rules during those troubled times.

Feelings ran very high during the war. Many friends and relatives never came back. I can remember being on the Carew to East Springfield bus one time during the war and a woman passenger was talking very loudly about how she wished the war would last a long time, because she had such a good job and would probably lose it once the boys were home. The bus driver was furious with her, slammed the brakes, and made her get off the bus.

After the war, most of us got married, started families and looked to the future. Though we all took different paths, we took a little bit of each other wherever we went.

Some of our life experiences would make rather good material for entertaining a TV audience without the sensationalism that TV producers deem as necessary.

Moments from childhood come to mind—the scarlet fever epidemic when the Health Department placed quarantine signs on our houses, forbidding anyone to come in or out. Bud Cabey chased the man from the Health Department for several blocks to let him know that he was friends with the rest of the people who were quarantined and could he please be quarantined too? And, he was.

Some of our dating experiences as teenagers are memorable and as funny as many current TV shows, there was the time I was sitting on the front porch swing with a new beau. My sister Marie and Ida Caron were in the house eavesdropping at the window, emitting belches and other embarrassing sounds and giggling. Needless to say, my date didn't stay too long! I didn't get mad but I did get even by calmly making some tea for all of us. After Ida and Marie drank their tea, I informed them that the milk I used in the tea was from the cat's dish! The gagging sounds they made were music to my ears.

Excerpts from our working lives would also be good TV fare. In the period following the Great Depression, the National Recovery Act had been enacted and most businesses had an NRA sign with a blue eagle in the window. One of these was Valley Farms Restaurant located in East Springfield across from the Westinghouse plant where Mary Wescott, my sister Marie and I worked as waitresses. Health Department standards were probably non-existent during this period of rebuilding the economy and cockroaches flourished in eating places.

A favorite memory is one of our waitress friends (who will remain nameless) filling soup bowls from a giant pot of soup using a ladle. Spotting a cockroach, she would slam it with the ladle and continue filling the bowls without missing a beat!

I distinctly remember Wednesday's special being soup, turkey with all the trimmings, pie and coffee for 25 cents. Little did the customers know what else was included in that bargain!

Though it was comical to watch, realistically, we couldn't waste time overreacting to bugs that everyone lived with when the Westinghouse workers had less than an hour to eat lunch. We knew our priorities!

These are just a few humorous events which are part of a long span of the friendships and families of ordinary people who lived through extraordinary times. There are hundreds of other stories and many people reading this could offer a few more. The consensus is that friends made a difference; they enhanced life's journey. I have a favorite saying from an unknown author that I framed for all of us. It sums up our friendship so well; "We may not have it altogether but together, we have it all."

Though time and death has thinned our ranks—World War II claimed a few friends, the Korean War took a younger sibling, others passed on due to illness, some are in nursing homes—as of this writing, Ida, Mary and I are in our 80s and have remained friends for 70 plus years.

My youngest son remarked recently that he hopes he and his friends live long enough to be in their 80s so they can hang out together like they did when they were teenagers. I hope so too as I've been there, done it, and highly recommend it!

Note: Rita Cabey Morris passed away in 2004. She was predeceased by her two friends, Ida and Mary.

THE GREATEST GENERATION

THE MIDNIGHT PROWL
Written by Frank Carey & Bud Cabey

Listen dear people and you will howl
When you hear of Father Carey's midnight prowl
Over he strolled to the Liberty Café
Just to tuck a few snifters away
There he met friends, Paddy, Ralph and Andy
When they got together, things were just dandy.
With each shot of beer and wine
Their troubles were magnified a thousand times
When the witching hour of twelve drew near
The boys were ready to cry in their beer.
Then homeward they trod their weary way
Two melancholy, two quite gay,
Said Paddy and Ralph, "The minutes are fleeting,
But, we'll see you at the "morning meeting"*
Said Pat to Andy, "My very good friend,
This running around must come to an end,
Our children are wayward, their ways they must mend.
They must come home early, and, I don't like their friends,
I think when we're home, we're a trifle henpecked
We are wasting away with abuse and neglect.
Then Pat and Andy say goodnight
Still brooding over their terrible plight............

The morning meeting was the Sunday morning
gathering at Andy Cabey's house.

THE LAST TO KNOW GENERATION

THE LAST TO KNOW GENERATION AT A GLANCE

In the early 1950s, Border Street and Laurence Streets, two of the streets that comprised the Lennox Platte—also known as the "patch" were paved and became official city streets. This removed the "private way dangerous" signs and provided residents with mail delivery to their homes, instead of walking down to the row of mailboxes on Carew Street.

Wilson Street—"the crossroads" which ran from Eddy to Nottingham Streets and crossed Laurence, Border, Middle, and Parallel street—was paved a few years later.

On trash day, trash men came into each yard or even into cellars to collect the trash. The garbage was a separate collection and the garbage men also walked into each yard to empty the garbage cans, which were usually in the ground.

Around 1954, the sixth grade classes at Liberty School were moved to Van Sickle due to overcrowding and were moved back the next fall when Pottenger School was built. Students carried their own desks down Carew Street to Liberty School.

Two Masses, one upstairs and one downstairs were always filled to capacity on Sundays at Our Lady of Hope Church. Once a week, after school, public school Catholic kids walked to CCD classes held at Our Lady of Hope School while Greek kids took the bus to St. George's Cathedral for Greek school.

The First Communion and Confirmation classes at Our Lady of Hope Church were huge. These classes included all public and parochial school kids, instructed by the Sisters of St. Joseph.

At the old Shriners Hospital, the young patients were brought outside in their wheelchairs and beds in warm weather.

General MacArthur's motorcade came down Liberty Street on its way to Chicopee to dedicate a memorial to his father, a native of Chicopee.

Laurence Street—1940s

Michael, Cheryl, Dick and Joan Morris

First Communion
1948—Joan Morris

Dick Morris &
George "Dickie" Bentley
Troop 51s Finest

Playtime on Laurence Street—1950

The ground is broken—Laurence Street was paved and
became a city street instead of a "Private Way Dangerous"
dirt road—Mid-1950s

Bits of Ben

My father, Ben Morris, had a heart of gold and was full of optimism. You could see it in his walk. He had a real spring in his step and looked on each day as a great adventure. Though short in stature, about 5' 7" tall, he seemed so big and tall and fearless in our young eyes.

Ben was not an educated man but, rather a product of the school of hard knocks. He worked for most of his life as a long haul truck driver with brief stints as a bus driver and a car salesman.

As kids we were astonished to hear an expression regarding someone who "swore like a truck driver." My truck driver father didn't curse or use bad language at home. He had his own unique vocabulary known only to him, his older brother Mike and God.

For example, if something was really special and top of the line, he would proudly say, "look at that, just like New York!"—probably a throwback to his younger days when he was a bellhop at some of the better hotels in New York City. If someone did something stupid, he or she was a "dunkey". My sister showed him the word donkey in the dictionary and pointed out that it was spelled with an 'o', not 'u'. Though he was pleased that one of his kids knew this fact and corrected him, he always reverted back to "dunkey" when the next "donkey" came along.

An endearment used with kids was "pumpernickelini" or "tyker." Any jobs that we had to do around the house had to be done using "elbow grease." Also, any cat we ever had was a "goozie." Other favorites were describing someone very nervy as having a "lot of moxie." and when someone tried to pull a fast one, he or she was definitely a "conniver" who needed a good kick in the "keister." A really clueless person was a "dizza wazza" and a cheapskate was a "chiseler." These colorful words still come to mind today when our paths cross with dunkeys or connivers.

This Lithuanian from Westfield opted to build a house on Hungry Hill as he had married an Irish girl from the hill and was very much at home there. He built our brick house part time when he wasn't driving a truck up and down the eastern seaboard. It was a huge undertaking and he was constantly harassed by the city inspectors. Those were the days when kickbacks from contractors were the norm—and he couldn't and wouldn't play that game.

One time when he was working on the second story, he received a notice from the city stating that he could not expand to the second floor until an inspection was done. Due to a large backlog, they couldn't tell him when it would be inspected, but until such time, he was to cease and desist from any further work. My father was so angry that he threw the hammer that was in his hand so far into the woods that he never found it again.

He got in his car and stormed downtown to City Hall with the notice in his hand. He barged into the building department and demanded that he be allowed to continue work on his house. Evidently, they listened because an inspection was forthcoming and work on the house continued without further delay until we were able to move in. Time was of the essence as he had a young family and the pressure of renting with small children weighed heavily on him so any unnecessary delays were not acceptable.

Ben worked hard and played hard. He had tremendous will power and very little patience. He was above all, a practical man, but could be very philosophical. I remember someone once talking to him about the importance of pride and things that he'd never do even if it meant cutting off one's nose to spite one's face, etc. I'll always remember my father's response to him, "Pride is good. I have pride, but I know when to bow my head."

A relative once confided to him about a drinking problem and reminded him that he too drank his share. My father agreed but he told the person, it's one thing to drink if you're in control, but when it's controlling you, it's time to stop. Amen, end of discussion.

He never hesitated to tell someone if their shoes needed a shine. He was religious about shined shoes in his own life and believed it spoke volumes about a person who didn't pay attention to the state of their shoes.

One of his greatest enjoyments was traveling, going to places he had never been. He was never happier than being on a trip and living the words of one of his favorite songs, "Far Away Places"—*I pray for the day I can get underway and look for those castles in Spain...*

Ben was very musical. He loved to sing and was a beautiful dancer. He went through his life constantly humming and he never traveled in his car without the radio blaring. One summer comes to mind when my daughter was taking art classes at the museum downtown. I had asked my Dad to pick her up as I was working. Beth fondly described waiting for her grandfather at the Quadrangle and hearing him coming in his station wagon with the windows rolled down and the radio blaring out golden oldies from "*The Music of*

Your Life" station. He loved all Irish music and would sing songs like *"Galway Bay"* and *"When Irish Eyes are Smiling"* with us and even tried Irish step dancing.

Ben was also a talented harmonica player. This was self-taught beginning at about ten years of age. He and two brothers, who also played harmonicas, were the entertainment at Morris family gatherings. When Ben played at home, his dog would howl along with him. He and my mother went on several trips with senior groups and Ben always carried his harmonica in his pocket and served as the entertainment.

In his later years, he joined a musical group of seniors called the Golden Age Harmonicats. This group had about a dozen members and they all played chromatic harmonicas. Ben was the secretary of the group and he booked all of their gigs. They usually played at nursing homes for the "old timers." In reality, most members of the group were older than the patients.

At age 86, Ben suffered a massive stroke which left him with speech aphasia. While he was recuperating in the hospital, one of the few things he was able to do was play his harmonica—which he did, much to the delight of the staff. He survived for five years and when he passed on his musical comrades came to his funeral with their harmonicas. On a cold, November day with light snow falling, there wasn't a dry eye at the cemetery as they played *"Now Is the Hour"* and other favorites.

Ben was a high-on-life people person, an eclectic though uncomplicated man who was married to the same woman for 65 years, had the best and brightest kids and grandkids (just ask him) and believed he was the luckiest man on earth to reach old age. His memory lives on in so many ways —a song on the radio from his era; anytime a harmonica is mentioned, the sturdy brick house that he built on pure nerve and the musical inclination of several of his grandchildren.

Unforgettable Jim Nash

In the early 1940s, my father was given a plot of land by my grandfather so he could build a house to accommodate his growing family. My father didn't have a house built he built a house, by himself, with a little help from friends. Though he had never tackled anything like this before, he had definite ideas about what a house had to have.

First of all, it had to be a brick house. The cellar had to have a main room with two separate side cellars. One side room was the coal cellar for coal deliveries through the window. The other was the vegetable cellar which was located under the front porch and had bins for fruit and vegetables. There had to be work benches in the cellar and the garage and an ironing board that folded into the wall of the kitchen. The outside of the house called for a clay base for the lawn and a rock garden.

One neighbor who was very helpful in building our house was Jim Nash, who lived a few doors down. My father never asked him for his help. Anytime Jim heard hammering, he appeared with his tools and his rudimentary knowledge of building, carpentry, electricity and plumbing and almost anything else and adopted the project as his own.

Jim was a local character, a Spanish-American war veteran, who lived by himself in a small dark house with no indoor plumbing. He had several outbuildings consisting of chicken coops, a workshop and an outhouse. It was hard to describe him other than being slightly built, stooped over with a very lined face and looking like he needed a GI bath most of the time.

His clothes were nondescript, although he once wore a suit and announced that he had a lady friend. What he lacked in style, he made up for in meat-and-potatoes basic know-how and experience and he successfully guided my father through this massive undertaking.

Jim had a drinking buddy and sidekick named George, another do-it-yourselfer. They were a colorful pair! On one occasion, George was cutting Jim's hair with a pair of scissors and missed and cut his ear—Jim let out a screech and chased George down the street with blood running out of his ear and an ax in his hands threatening to kill him. George was the finisher. He did the wallpapering and painting. However, if he did too much imbibing before a job, one had better hope that there weren't stripes on the paper or anything else that had to be lined up.

Because of the way Jim walked, bent over and looking downward, he found many items on the ground and once gave my mother a gift of a whole box of rusty hairpins that he had found on his travels. My mother thanked him for the gift and discreetly disposed of them.

Jim raised chickens and periodically killed one for dinner. His method was to cut off the chicken's head and have it run around headless until it dropped. As young kids we were horrified to witness this!

Jim lived to be a ripe old age though his actual age was unknown. He was one of those larger-than-life characters, a survivor with an unorthodox style and a big heart who helped many people along the way by offering his "seat of the pants" knowledge whenever the occasion arose.

ANTHONY IN THE ATTIC
Creative Summer Discipline

Growing up on the upper Carew Street section of Hungry Hill in Springfield, Massachusetts in the 1940s and 1950s was practically country living.

Each season of the year generated various pastimes for the large number of kids in the area but summers were especially memorable. Even now, whenever summer is approaching, my thoughts wander to other summers when Liberty School rang the final bell in late June to signify the start of summer vacation. What a euphoric feeling that was! The whole summer looming ahead with no schoolwork and no responsibilities, just pure freedom all day long until the streetlights came on at dusk. That was our signal to go in the house.

Our summers were tranquil pastoral scenes with dirt roads, huge vegetable gardens, blueberry bushes, apple and pear trees, a chestnut tree in Uncle Andrew's yard, a mulberry tree in front of Mrs. Wilbur's house (invaluable for the silkworm projects in school), Mrs. Bentley's grape arbor loaded with purple concord grapes and her thick blackberry patch. The air was sheer perfume emanating from the trellis in Grandpa Cabey's yard which was weighed down with roses as well as his giant peony and hollyhock bushes and those tiny, intoxicating lily of the valley plants.

Other than pestering our mothers, we were mostly seen and not heard as we drifted through idyllic barefoot days playing on swings, building huts in the grove which had numerous white birch trees (note to Robert Frost, we too were swingers of birches), and climbing our favorite tree next to Wilbur's driveway. On several occasions, Mr. Wilbur had to rescue his daughter Judy and my sister Cheryl when they lost their nerve and couldn't make it down the tree.

We also rode bikes, had pickup games of baseball and basketball, played hopscotch, roller skated with key skates, joined the summer reading club at the library, watched the Italian men play bocce at the Marconi Club and tried to catch a glimpse of a bride at the numerous Saturday wedding receptions.

By late July and August, the wild blueberries were ready to pick and we all participated, filling glass milk bottles with blueberries in anticipation of the pies that my mother would bake with our bounty.

We were avid card players involved in games of Go Fish, Slapjack, poker and canasta and board games like Sorry and Monopoly. A real treat on very hot days was to walk to Emily Bill playground in the North End, just past the imaginary boundary line of Hungry Hill, to swim in the public pool.

On the frequent occasions when kids would be kids and do silly things or act unruly or argumentative, my family's way of dealing with these outbursts was original. My siblings and I were indoctrinated at an early age to the infamous Anthony who, supposedly, lived in Grandpa Cabey's attic.

Anthony was a figment of someone's imagination whose sole purpose in life was to make sure kids minded their parents and behaved well. Though we never actually saw him, all it took to strike fear in our hearts was Aunt Marie (aka Nonnie) to open the door to the attic stairs and yell, "A-a-a-an-thony, there's some kids down here who aren't behaving!"

Sometimes we would sit on our front steps across the street and stare at the attic window through the trees and swear that we saw a dark figure at the window. What we later discovered was that the grownups in the family, to dispel any doubts about Anthony's existence, had actually constructed a dummy out of straw, dressed him in Grandpa's clothes and a soft hat and sat him in the front window. It did the trick—we were scared witless!

The only adult to whom we dared voice our anxiety about Anthony was Grandpa Cabey who always assured us with his slight Clare brogue that Anthony was not a bad fellow and he usually stayed upstairs and minded his business (whatever that was). "Let ye kids be good and he'll never bother you atall, atall," he'd say.

As we got older and wiser, Anthony became less of a threat to us and more of a comic relief. For instance, whenever any of the neighbors returned from a vacation, they were likely to find Anthony in their bed or sitting on their porch or front steps surrounded by beer bottles. This was a neighborhood where camaraderie and good clean fun was always present and everyone enjoyed their turn with Anthony.

I'm not sure exactly when Anthony met his demise and lost some of his straw, as well as his reputation. It was at some point after Grandpa Cabey died and after some of the neighbors had moved away.

Modern psychologists would probably not approve of this form of discipline based on fear but our little corner of Springfield was not a complicated place. The end and the times justified the means and the memories are priceless!

LIBERTY SCHOOL
Lessons for Life

One of the plusses of living on Hungry Hill during the 1940s and 1950s was the quality of the public schools in the neighborhood. One school in particular, Liberty School on Carew Street, taught much more than the three Rs to its young student body. Liberty is one of the smallest elementary schools in Springfield. Despite its size, it served as the hub of the upper Carew Street section of Hungry Hill during that time period.

In those days of neighborhood schools, everyone walked to school. It was rare to have a mother that drove a car. For the students, this meant gaining independence and responsibility at an early age. You got yourself to school on time and, if you were late, you stayed after school.

One advantage of the micro educational system in place during those years was the sense of community that evolved. Open House nights at Liberty were a sea of familiar faces and camaraderie. The teachers at Liberty School were like members of an extended family. Most were unmarried, spent decades on the job and knew every home situation. Teaching in those days was one of the few career options for talented women. The principal, Miss Sheehan, and teachers like McMahon, Elliot, Derby, Dougan, West, Rhodes, Smith and Kaplan represented some of the finest people and dedicated educators that Springfield can only hope to see again.

The tiny auditorium at Liberty served many functions. During school hours, it was used for assemblies and a lunchroom for those that brought lunches from home. There were no hot lunches. After school and evenings, the auditorium was reserved for Brownie meetings, Cub Scout

74

meetings, PTA meetings, minstrel shows, food sales, etc.

Spirtuality had a presence at Liberty. Long before the Supreme Court banned prayer in the schools, every day in every classroom began with opening exercises consisting of a Bible reading usually the 23rd Psalm, the Pledge of Allegiance and sometimes a patriotic hymn. It was a comfortable, predictable way to start each day.

Thrift was practiced and encouraged. "A penny saved is a penny earned" would best describe the student banking program run by SIS Bank. It was a very adult thing to have your own passbook and be able to add to it on bank day, which was usually on Tuesday.

Academic excellence was reinforced with events like spelling bees. Miss Kaplan offered an ice cream sundae for the person who had the most "bb's" (the most papers displayed on the bulletin board). At one point when there was overcrowding in the upper grades, several of the highest achieving students were double promoted to the next grade.

Discipline was aimed towards character building rather than punishment. One creative form of discipline practiced only at Liberty School was to be assigned to the courtyard to pull weeds. Liberty has a small open courtyard in the center of the school with a fountain in the middle of a concrete wading pool. There was rarely water in the pool, so, weeds would grow up through the cracks in the cement. The punishment part was having other students see you laboring in the courtyard. My brother Michael frequently worked on building character.

Competition in track and field events was part of life at Liberty School. Every spring, a citywide field day was

75

held when every grammar school in the city competed in events like relay races, broad jumping, basketball throws, etc. Excitement ran high in the quest for the coveted blue ribbons.

The arts flourished at Liberty School. The music program included choral singing, studying great composers and learning to play instruments, as well as yearly trips to hear the Springfield Symphony perform "The Nutcracker" or "Peter and the Wolf." Drama was available in the form of Christmas pageants and Miss Rhodes' puppet program where students made puppets, sewed clothes for them, learned to work them with strings and put on a play every year.

Volunteerism was alive and well at Liberty. Many of the boys delivered milk in bottles to the classrooms. After the milk break, the bottles had to be picked up and rinsed. Volunteers were always needed after school to clean blackboards and clap erasers outside. The safety patrol was second to none— a real no-nonsense corps of students with their required clean white belts and badges.

Admittedly, life was less complicated then. It was a time when respect for authority and playing by the rules was the norm which provided a security of sorts. Liberty School, then, was part of a less diverse system that operated under the assumption that all of society had the same goals and held the same things dear. Leaders in the education field "steered by the stars" and, inadvertently, instilled a value system along with a solid academic foundation.

CAREW & NEWBURY
A Multicultural Marketplace

Hungry Hill in the 1950s had numerous stores and small businesses. Armory Street had Schermerhorn's Fish Market, where everybody gravitated on meatless Fridays, and Liberty Street had the A&P, Liberty Bakery and a few small markets.

The most concentrated selection of stores, however, could be found at the intersection of Carew and Newbury Streets which were run by a diverse group of merchants. This mini marketplace consisted of:

Fulton's Market – owned and operated by Louie Zointz, a Jewish butcher and grocery entrepreneur. Call-in orders were delivered cheerfully by Al Giroux. Customers could run up tabs and pay when they could—an anchor for 20 plus years.

Louie's Barber Shop – the Italian barber. A male domain—the boys in the neighborhood were regulars. The girls always wondered about it but rarely went in, except for an occasional brave female who experimented with a barbershop hair cut.

Jimmy's Spa – a once elegant soda fountain and ice cream parlor with marble counters and booths. In our family, when we learned to tie our shoes, we were rewarded with an ice cream soda at Jimmy's. Jimmy was an older man from Greece with a leathery face and prominent bags under his eyes. He had a young wife, Tula, from Greece, who worked at the store. I can remember being fascinated with her bushy hair and pale skin with a spot of dark rouge on each cheek.

Doris Kakley Flower Shop – Doris decorated our lives. Her striking window displays were the jewels on the crown of this little cluster of stores. This fine French lady was a good neighbor who said it with flowers at all of the weddings, funerals and other times in our lives.

Sheehan's Tavern – no women or kids ever went into Peter Sheehan's establishment, one of the few Irish businesses. The door was often left open and, walking by we could hear the sound of clinking glasses and the buzz of numerous conversations in the dark, smoky interior full of shadowy figures.

Carew Pharmacy – Dave and Jack Goldberg, Jewish brothers who dispensed goodwill along with prescriptions. The soda fountain was a great place to have a vanilla coke. Dave was the businessman and could be firm when ejecting kids who spent hours reading comic books but never bought one.

Jack was a gentleman as well as a gentle man—a kind soft spoken soul who allowed families to run up tabs for prescription medicines. One scene that always comes to mind is my brothers bringing a wagonload of soda bottles to the back door of the pharmacy to cash them in for deposit money so we would have the 16 cents admission to Liberty Theater and a nickel for Necco Wafers.

McNamara's Package Store – another off-limits place for kids, part of the landscape for decades and, until recently, one that was still in operation by the same people. It always amazed us how such an Irish-sounding place was actually owned by the Josephs, a Lebanese family in the area.

Ed Sullivan's Hardware – another business with an Irish name—massive amounts of small hardware items and a good place to buy a key for roller skates and to have ice skates sharpened.

Bell Dee Distributors – the silent partner of the marketplace. A storefront office and warehouse for whatever it was they distributed. I don't ever recall seeing any activity there but there must have been something going on as they were there for decades.

Joe's Variety – last, but not least, a little further down at Middle Street and Carew was Joe's Variety, the milk, bread and penny candy store run by an Italian family. Joe, Cora and little Joe always provided a running dialogue while we agonized over which penny candies to buy.

Though we were blissfully unaware of it at the time, we were fortunate to have experienced such a potpourri of ethnic flavors by merchants who genuinely cared about the neighborhood and its people.

DR. HAGGERTY'S WAITING ROOM

For many years, there were three doctors living on Hungry Hill with offices in their homes—Doctors Greaney and Conway on Carew Street and Dr. Haggerty on Ledyard Street. A fourth doctor came later, Dr. Blackmer on Governor Street.

Our family doctor was Dr. Francis Haggerty on Ledyard Street, a short, amiable man who wrote the book on bedside manner. He was a general practitioner whose wide range of expertise included all types of internal medicine as well as obstetrics, gynecology, dermatology, psychology, gastroenterology, stress management techniques, etc., etc... and, he made house calls.

All of the children in our family were delivered by Dr. Haggerty. One of my mother's fondest memories is Dr. Haggerty visiting her at Mercy Hospital after delivering my brother, her first child. He informed her that the nuns were disappointed—they thought Morris was a Jewish name which would mean a circumcision ceremony with wine!

The few times I ever went to see Dr. Haggerty during office hours were memorable. His waiting room had leather chairs and smelled like my grandfather's shaving cream. The waiting room was usually full. There were people dozing in chairs, several nuns, and numerous others who weren't really sick but were there to chat and find out the latest gossip from Dr. Haggerty, especially if he had made a recent trip to Ireland.

No one ever had an appointment; it was first come, first served. Dr. Haggerty would come out to the waiting room, ask who was next and, when it was your turn, you followed him down a narrow hall to his office, which had a door that opened outward—so you had to step back so the door could swing open.

He constantly hummed a tuneless repertoire as he was talking to you. He was always able to quickly diagnose and treat my ailments, tonsillitis, an allergic reaction to wool, German Measles, etc.

Many years later, my future husband and I made an office visit to Dr. Haggerty to have blood tests done for our marriage license. I distinctly recall him taking a sample of my blood first and then informing me that my fiance's blood would be much thicker and redder than mine because he was all Irish and I was only half and, he was right, my blood looked almost bluish by comparison!

The last time I saw Dr. Haggerty was in the late sixties when my two year old son had hit his head falling against the coffee table and had been treated at the emergency room. I went to Dr. Haggerty to have the stitches removed but he was not able to help me. He explained that his hands shook badly and he couldn't do it. Not too long after that, I heard that he was in a nursing home and eventually passed away.

Dr. Haggerty practiced what the holistic movement is striving for today—the ability to connect with the patient and treat the whole person. I'm not sure if we'll ever see a doctor like Francis Haggerty again but, if by some miracle we do, I doubt that he or she will make house calls!

THE LAST TO KNOW GENERATION

AND THERE USED TO BE A THEATER...

The Liberty Theater, a modest two-story building on Liberty Street, opened in 1928. During its 30-year existence, it was a major source of entertainment for Hungry Hill residents. My mother remembers getting a whole set of dishes, one at a time on Wednesday evenings at the Liberty during the 1930s.

Though there were numerous downtown movie theaters in the 1940s and 1950s, for convenience and price, you couldn't beat having a theater right in the neighborhood. The Liberty was the Hollywood connection for so many young impressionable Hungry Hill residents. For the bargain price of sixteen cents, we were transported to another place.

Nothing could compare with watching a cowboy and Indian battle and hearing a bugle signify the arrival of the cavalry. Everyone in the place would cheer and applaud! We were all equally delighted at seeing good triumph over evil! My sisters and cousin, who were diehard cowboy fans, were so inspired by the cowboy serials that they would gallop all the way home—across the A&P parking lot, down Phoenix Terrace, across Nottingham Street, down Wilson to Laurence Street, a pretty good gallop even for young energetic kids.

I can still remember the incredible noise level at a typical Saturday matinee and the theater manager, a short man with red hair, who would stop the movie, walk on stage and warn the crowd of young moviegoers that he wasn't going to run the movie until it was quiet. He was usually booed and popcorn boxes were thrown at the stage. He would finally give up and start the movie again.

My love of musicals, which is still alive and well, began at the Liberty with MGM musicals, 1950s vintage. Another regular feature in those days was the newsreels – "The Eyes and Ears of the World." I didn't fully appreciate the value of these Movietone newsreels as a kid, but home television sets were scarce and, unless you read the newspapers well and listened to radio newscasts—neither of which appealed to any kids I knew—these newsreels were the sole source of information as to what was going on in the world. This concept is hard to imagine in the information age we now live in where we're inundated with news 24 hours a day.

Several years ago I saw a Woody Allen movie, "Purple Rose of Cairo," which was a black-and-white film featuring Mia Farrow whose character went to the movies almost daily to escape her unhappy life. At one point, she was the only person in the theater and an actor on the screen looked out into the dark theater and asked her if she wanted to join them and she actually walked into the screen! This brought me back to being a kid at the Liberty and the many times I wanted to do that very thing as I sat there watching the glamorous Hollywood world, wishing I could be part of it.

The theater building was sold in the late 1950s to Inland Marine & Hardware Company who planned to use the screen for sales purposes and boat displays. The building today consists of a few small stores and is hardly recognizable as the former entertainment "Mecca" of Hungry Hill movie fans.

RITUALS FROM ANOTHER ERA

Bless me father, for I have sinned…

In the 1950s confession, now known as reconciliation, was a predictable regular occurrence on Saturday afternoons at Our Lady of Hope Church. In those days, the main church and the basement church held Masses, both of which were filled on Sundays. Confessions were heard in the lower church and every Saturday, there were at least three priests hearing confessions, sometimes four, and with the possible exception of Father Power's confessional, there were 3 or 4 rows of kids waiting for their turn to confess their sins. I can remember one of the favorites being Father Price, a soft-spoken kind man.

It's been one week since my last confession and these are my sins…

I remember my sister and I, along with assorted cousins and friends walking to Our Lady of Hope Church for confession almost every Saturday. On the way, we tried to get our sins organized and determine which evil deeds constituted mortal or venial sins. They ranged from getting mad at someone to taking the Lord's name in vain or eating meat on a Friday or —heaven forbid—missing Mass. My sister would be close to tears before she got there exclaiming, "I've only got 4 sins and I'm scared!"

I detest all my sins because I dread the loss of heaven and the pains of hell…

On many occasions, Father Power would make us move from the rows for the more popular priests to his section. More than once, Father would leave the confessional and ask who came with the girl who was crying in his confessional. I was furious when I had to claim her as my sister. Another sister was afraid that the priest would punish her for telling a sibling that she was an "h-i-t." One cousin was so nervous that he told the priest that it had been 3 years since his last confession instead of 3 weeks and the priest left the confessional to urge whoever had come with this young man to convince him to go to confession more often.

It took a pretty brave young soul to actually choose Father Power as his or her confessor. His ways were well-known among us penitents. He would first ask you if you went to parochial school and if the answer was no, he would inquire why, as he thought all good Catholics went to parochial school. So, even before we started, we were totally unnerved because we were off on the wrong foot being public school Catholics. We usually ended up with a huge amount of prayers to say for penance including a good act of contrition, not to mention a deep sense of relief.

I firmly resolve with the help of thy grace to confess my sins, to do penance and to amend my life…

Once we were given absolution, we were a more light-hearted group on the walk home. By today's standards, it could be argued that this spiritual cleansing was based on fear and was not healthy. It was definitely based on fear but those were less complicated times. The fabric of our young lives was made up of home, school and church, all equally influential. Limits were set for us and confession made us accountable for our own behavior knowing that if we crossed that line, eventually, we would have to tell a priest and do some form of penance.

Making sacrifices during Lent was another tradition that inspired us to reach for loftier heights and become better people. It was hard to imagine how giving up candy for Lent accomplished this, except that self-discipline can be character-building and Lenten sacrifices were personal choices made at a young age. For the determined few who managed to stick to their Lenten vows, Easter Sunday was truly a day to rejoice in more ways than one. AMEN!

The Last to Know Generation

Laurence Street's Big Bang!

Fourth of July celebrations back in the 1950s were done on a small scale in our little corner of Hungry Hill. They consisted of family picnics enhanced with sparklers, salutes, rockets and cap guns. My family looked forward to my father bringing us fireworks from New Jersey, one of his stops as a long haul truck driver.

One year, my Dad brought us a bag of cherry bombs, as well as the usual small strings of salutes and sparklers. The morning of July 4 was uneventful. My two brothers, along with assorted friends spent the morning lighting the cherry bombs and salutes, using tin cans and other creative ways to enhance the noise. They enjoyed dropping salutes into the storm drains on the edge of the street, which amplified the sound.

Then someone got the idea to drop a salute down a manhole. So they did, and when it exploded, chaos ensued! The manhole cover, which was very heavy, flipped over from the impact of the blast and we could hear windows breaking in various houses on the street. Two of the kids who were standing about 20 feet away in a vacant lot started running and screaming "my eyes." Their hair, face and eyes were totally singed! I sat on my bike paralyzed with fear! Neighbors were emptying out of their houses!

Just prior to this, my brother Michael had the ingenious idea to insert a cherry bomb into the straw body of a headless, discarded doll and blow it to pieces! So, he inserted a cherry bomb, lit it and stepped back to watch. Nothing happened. Assuming this was a dud or the flame went out, he picked up the doll to investigate and it exploded in his hand! My parents were treating his badly burned hand when the new

87

explosion occurred and shook their brick house.

Within minutes, the street was swarming with people! One of the neighbors said they just heard a news bulletin on the local television station about an explosion on Laurence Street. Cruisers, an ambulance and gas company trucks crowded the area. Another neighbor who worked for the gas company went down into the manhole and confirmed that there was a gas leak.

The two injured kids were taken to the hospital and treated for burns. Fortunately, there was no damage to their eyes. Gas company crews worked on the leak and eventually, calm was restored.

My mother confiscated the remaining fireworks, cherry bombs, salutes, etc., from my brothers and, at a later date, actually dug a hole and buried them! Needless to say, from that time on, July 4th celebrations became quieter. Sparklers and cap guns became the extent of our noise making and even then, we were cautioned as to their use.

THE LAST TO KNOW GENERATION

MARCONI CLUB

The Marconi Club has been located on Hungry Hill for more than 70 years. It was named for Guglielmo Marconi, the Italian inventor who was a pioneer in transatlantic radio transmissions.

Located on a corner that encompasses Parallel Street, Wilson Street and Middle Street, the Marconi Club was a popular hall for Hungry Hill weddings and parties. The Italian men playing bocce were part of the sights and sounds of growing up on Laurence Street, one street over. As surprising as having an Italian club on Hungry Hill was the discovery that Marconi, though born in Italy, had something in common with many of us in the neighborhood—his mother was Irish!

The Marconi Club was a good neighbor for many years. As a social club in an exclusively residential neighborhood, it seemed to coexist without problems. Even though there was a bar downstairs, I don't ever remember hearing about any disturbances or complaints from neighbors because of it.

There used to be plum trees on the property that neighborhood boys were known to climb now and then. The young girls in the neighborhood loved to stand at the fence on Saturdays when there was a wedding to see if we could catch a glimpse of the bride and sometimes, we were offered a piece of wedding cake with tiny silver balls in the frosting! Right into the 1970s, my youngest brother and his friends were allowed to use the parking lot to play street hockey.

There were parties held at the club on a regular basis, which my parents and many others on the street attended. On one legendary occasion, probably in the mid 50s, most of the Laurence Street neighbors were attending a party at the club At some point in the evening, my aunt, who we called Nonnie, wanted to get her husband Smalley home as he had imbibed more than he could handle.

My aunt never drove a car, nor did her husband so she went around to some of the other men—my father, her brother Billy, her cousin Bud and others—and asked them to take Smalley home. They were all having a great time and they told her to leave him alone, they would take him home later. Not to be deterred, Nonnie marched one street over through our backyard to her house and brought her wheelbarrow back to the club. She somehow managed to get Smalley into the wheelbarrow and wheeled him home by herself! The language that came out of that sweet Irish lady was unbelievable!

There have been many changes in the neighborhood. There are houses where there were once vacant lots and open spaces around the club. I'm not sure when the club started to lose its appeal for wedding receptions. It might have been at about the time when it changed hands and lost its ethnic flavor. The bocce courts are now silent and neglected and a different crowd frequents the bar, though the upstairs is still used for local parties and gatherings.

When I pass by there now, in my mind, I still hear the clicking sound of bocce games on summer evenings and recall the days when the Marconi Club made our little neighborhood more worldly by its Italian influence.

The Last to Know Generation

Riding with Rainbow School

I came from a family of seven children and family car trips were raucous events. Sometime in the mid 1950s, my truck driver father bought a used nine-passenger station wagon, a vintage 1949 or 1950 Ford with wooden doors that had "Rainbow School" painted on them in italic lettering. It had previously belonged to a local nursery school, which still exists today. My father would never dream of having the name removed. Not only would it cost money, it might affect the nice finish of the wood. Naturally, a station wagon loaded with kids that had a school name on it drew attention wherever we went. We were constantly asked if we were students at the school and what kind of school it was, etc. As an adolescent girl and almost a teenager, I found these questions extremely embarrassing—but then again, everything was at that age.

My father tended to buy trucks for his many business ventures, so we were thrilled that we actually had a car to go places in. Going places in those days consisted of trips that were pretty close by – church, shopping, visiting relatives in Westfield, Sunday outings at Look Park in Northampton, or visiting the Boy Scout camp in Woronoco, where my brother was a staff member. One memorable vacation was at Cedar Lake in Sturbridge, when our cat was included in the mix and added to the clutter and chaos inside the vehicle. An occasional trip to the Connecticut shore rounded out our itinerary of road trips. Though it looked better than a truck, it was as solid as any truck we ever rode in. We were once involved in an accident when a car rammed into us, but no one was hurt or even shook up.

The noise level on these trips must have been incredible —siblings fighting for the seat near the window, punching one another when the opportunity arose, the cat yowling, etc. "Go with the flow" must have originated with my parents, who calmly and serenely endured the chaos and noise of these car trips without batting an eye—or one of us! Instead, they would play the radio and sing along to the music of their lives.

One advantage of looking like a school came to light on our Sunday outings at Look Park Prior to the station wagon, our only vehicle was a large half-trailer sized truck. We all sat in the back with the food and chairs, etc., and were able to stretch out on blankets for the ride home. As we were weekly visitors in the summer, we got to know many of the park personnel, especially the park police. Instead of parking in the designated lot, one officer named Vic used to jump on the running board of the truck and escort us over to Grove 24, centrally located near a stream. This had become our personal picnic grove by squatters' rights or eminent domain or, more likely, by someone reserving it every week.

Once we changed our mode of transportation to Rainbow School, it was even easier to get preferential status and an escort through the park to unload our paraphernalia. Onlookers were satisfied that this special treatment was because we were a school. This may not seem like a big deal, but with a truck or carload of kids, picnic supplies, coolers, food, etc., it was a break and gave us a degree of importance, at least in our minds. During our many activities at the park, other picnic goers would smile and tell us how nice that our school had this outing for us. My reaction was to smile and nod my head and caution my sister to do likewise.

Rainbow School lasted for many years – my father used it for his job at that time, which was a salesman and distributor for a trading stamp company. Our garage served as a warehouse for premium redemption items, which he delivered to customers in several New England states. So when the car wasn't loaded with kids and a cat for family outings, the seats were folded down and it was packed with premiums for trading stamp savers.

Amazingly, some 50 years later, I answered my phone and heard someone ask, "Is this Rainbow School?" I was so taken back that I just mumbled, "No." Afterwards, I thought of so many snappy comebacks like "it used to be Rainbow School" or "we all graduated" or some such comment. I'll probably never have that opportunity again.

When people complain about American cars and lament that "they don't make them like they used to," I think of Rainbow School and I have to agree. It was a roomy, comfortable, dependable mode of transportation and like the energizer bunny of today, it kept on going!

THE LAST TO KNOW GENERATION

A BUS RIDE INTO THE PAST

Picture it. Hungry Hill in the mid-Fifties—it's Saturday and a group of youngsters, early teens and younger, decide to spend the day downtown. Step back in time and join us as we wait in front of Liberty School for the Springfield Street Railway bus—Belmont line. We don't have to wait long; it's an efficient bus system. We can easily find a seat when we board the bus.

The familiar landscape passes by at each stop along Carew Street, beginning with Carew and Newbury, where the "corner bunch" hangs out. At least seven or eight young men stand around and pass the time in front of the Carew Pharmacy.

We then approach Bottle Park at Carew and Liberty where we spot a different group of males, all ages, gathered presumably to kibitz and hash out the problems of the day. As we pass this intersection, a quick glance down Liberty Street assures us that familiar landmarks like Liberty Methodist Church, Vezina's Drug Store, Loughran's Market, the A&P store, the Liberty Theater and the Liberty Branch Library are just where they should be.

We proceed past the two- and three-family houses lining both sides of Carew Street, past Leahy's Market up to Carew and Armory, where Our Lady of Hope Church and school, the Van Horn Spa, Schmerhorn's Fish Market and Wenger's Bakery coexist peacefully and service the same people daily. Next, Shriner's Hospital, the pleasant looking brick building where, in warm weather, one can see the young patients with their casts and wheelchairs on the patios.

94

We then cruise past Mercy Hospital with its once grand old buildings. Then, coming up on the right is the Russian Orthodox Church with its unique gold domes and crosses.

Then, the wonderful aroma of fresh baked bread from the Bond Bakery permeates the bus. We've now reached the north end of Main Street, a thriving community within itself, where we pass numerous markets and food stores, Royal Meat Market, Grower's Outlet and Stop & Shop. There is also Mr. Downey's shoe store, where my father bought us Sundial shoes, several upscale women's clothing stores, a wallpaper and paint store, and the Star Candy soda fountain, the Adams Table, the Hotel Charles and Day and Night Hatter.

Once we pass by the Arch and the Paramount Theater, we've arrived! What a range of stores await us from the Five & Ten stores (three of them), to Steiger's, Forbes & Wallace, J.C. Penney, Johnson's Book Store, Muriels, Peerless and numerous other small ladies clothing stores.

Our options are endless. When we get hungry, there's the Nutte Goode Tea Room, the Colony on Bridge Street, Steiger's Tea Room, Top of the Town Restaurant or the fountain at Woolworth's.

But first, let's check out the latest 45 records by stopping in to see Loretta at Kresge's Five & Ten store. After browsing through the records and checking out the hodgepodge of items that Kresge's had to offer, we go across the street to Neisner's and have our picture taken at the photo booth.

Then, after many trips up and down the escalators at

Steiger's and Forbes & Wallace, a visit to the toy department at Johnson's Book Store and a lot of window shopping up and down Main Street, we have a burger at the Colony.

At this point, we're out of money, so we decide to wait for the Carew to East Springfield bus, which will bring us home. At the bus stop in front of Steiger's, there's usually a bus every 15 or 20 minutes. Even if the bus is crowded and we have to stand for awhile, by the time we get to Mercy Hospital, there are seats available.

As the bus climbs Hungry Hill, we decide to stop at Our Lady of Hope Church as we're just in time for Saturday afternoon confessions. No Saturday Masses in those days! After our spiritual cleansing, we walk home, straight up Carew Street, turning off at Nottingham Street. Then we cut down Wilson Street, past the Marconi Club, where a wedding reception is taking place, and we catch a glimpse of the bride.

We part company as we head to our respective houses just in time for supper. Here we chat about our day with the rest of the family, blissfully unaware of our place in time and oblivious to the certainty that days like this were destined to disappear into memory along with much of the landscape. The unheard of concept of giant shopping malls open every night and even on Sundays would have boggled our 1950s mindset!

The Last to Know Generation

Newlyweds on the Hill

As I lived on Hungry Hill all my life, it seemed natural when I got married to look for an apartment in my comfort zone. We found a great apartment on the first floor of a beautiful old house on Wolcott Street with shiny maple floors, a ceramic brick fireplace with pillars, stained glass trim on the windows, a built in hutch cabinet and a large wraparound front porch. As we both worked downtown, this was an ideal location, close to both of our offices. We lived there for several years.

As well as I thought I knew Hungry Hill, in this section, there were everyday events bordering on folklore that I never would have known about on Laurence Street.

One example was the Emerald Package Store right around the corner on Liberty Street, which not only provided the sacramental wine for Our Lady of Hope Church but, rumor had it, they sold Mass cards! This store was run by a craggy Irishman with a brogue. He reminded me of the Squire Danaher character in the movie, "The Quiet Man." There were always assorted men hanging around, passing time with the owner. Anytime I walked in, everyone would stop talking and the owner would impatiently ask in a loud voice, "What do you want, lady?" He preferred male customers.

My husband was on such good terms with the owner that on occasion, when he didn't have the price of a six pack of beer, he would purchase the beer with silver dollars from his collection and request the owner hang on to them for a few days until he had some paper money to swap for the silver. Once, I actually asked the owner if it was true that Mass cards were sold there. He asked, "Do ya want one?" I guess I could have bought one then but, at the time, I was just trying to confirm whether the rumor was true.

We met some very interesting people while living there. Our landlord's daughter, who lived upstairs with her parents, was Miss Springfield that year. A Jewish family lived one house down. The father, Max, was a proponent of recycling. He went around on trash days and picked up items on tree belts for resale. This may not seem like a great line of work but he sent his two children to very prestigious colleges from this humble endeavor. We lived next door to the Garveys, a well-known Hungry Hill family with seven or eight kids, always an action-packed place. Across the street was a cousin of my mother's and the two Shea families, very fine people, who still reside there. We blended in easily with this diverse group and had our first child there.

The house we lived in was one of several on the street taken by eminent domain because of highway construction. While we looked for another place, we didn't pay rent for several months as it had become the property of the redevelopment authority. All but four houses were taken for Route 291 including the Emerald Package Store, which relocated further down on Liberty Street near Bottle Park.

Historically, progress always has a price tag. When neighbors are relocated and houses are torn down, the landscape isn't the only thing that changes. The character and the charm of an area disappear into memory and what memories they are! I'm glad they were part of my time on Hungry Hill.

HIS NAME WAS MICHAEL
Reflections on a Shooting Star

Shooting star: *a bright, brilliant, brief streak of light that speeds through the atmosphere and lights up the night sky.*

Michael was born and brought up in a kinder, gentler era on Hungry Hill in Springfield, Massachusetts, at a time when no one locked doors and many of the streets in that part of the city, including Laurence Street were dirt roads. It was the best of times for an energetic high-on-life kid.

There were numerous playmates with the same spirited agenda—riding bikes, building huts, taunting the girls with grass snakes or homemade sling shots, catching grasshoppers and fireflies in jars, climbing trees in the grove, picking blueberries near the Marconi Club, playing baseball and basketball in the field and twilight games of "kick the can," which was basically hide-and-seek with a tin can.

The years came and went with traditional seasonal activities where Michael's rich imagination took center stage. He would color Easter eggs his way by dipping an egg in every color and making a mongrel. He would be the one setting off salutes and other noisemakers at 4th of July picnics.

Endless summer days included building a hut among the white birch trees in the grove, raiding Mrs. Bentley's blackberry bushes and grape arbor, crushing choke cherries to make juice which he cajoled his sisters into drinking and hanging around Mrs. Wilbur's back door on the days that she made doughnuts.

Another regular ritual was collecting soda bottles in his

99

wagon to bring to the back door of the Carew Pharmacy and cashing them in for enough money (16 cents) to go to the Liberty Theater, our little neighborhood's Hollywood connection. Bobbing for apples at the annual Halloween party in his family's cellar and gathering all the discarded Christmas trees on the street to make a huge New Year's bonfire ended each year with his usual flair.

He once cut a record with his very musical father, singing oldies like "Cruising Down the River" and "Careless Hands." He was always moving, always thinking, always popular and always correcting people who called him Mike or Mickey. "My name is Michael," he would say. This assertion seemed to confirm his importance and his place in the scheme of things.

As he grew into adolescence, baseball in the field was replaced with official Little League ball for Our Lady of Hope Church, but the field was still great for ragtag baseball for every age or to shoot a few baskets or just fool around playing tag with numerous friends. Teachers as well as classmates were drawn to him. One junior high art teacher kept in touch with him for over 25 years.

He was a natural tease—he knew exactly which buttons to push, especially where his sisters were concerned. They were always good for a chase. Even in those days of kids going to bed early, he wasn't satisfied until he crept into his sisters' room at least once a night and made scary noises and they'd scream at him. No one had to tell them his name was Michael!

In high school, his popularity soared! Good looking, impeccable dresser, highly intelligent, contagious sense of humor, avid reader, class president, football player, class couple—he had it all! A part time job at a soda fountain only added to his charisma. Again, there was no shortage of friends. He possessed a magnetism that drew people of all ages. He was impressive! He impressed! Those years many called him Mike, but his name was Michael!

Shortly after graduation from high school, Michael interviewed and was hired by Monsanto Chemical Co. They too were impressed. This was the beginning of a career that took him all over the world, living in Europe and various large cities in the United States. He eventually married and had a wife and two sons to be proud of, a beautiful home, a global agenda. His good fortune was unstoppable...or so it seemed.

For 35 years, in his own words, he played the "corporate game" to the max. He embraced a philosophy, a work ethic and a lifestyle at a very young age. The downside of this youthful indoctrination and instant success was there were no "lean years"—no time to develop a mature value system or spiritual base, attributes that serve as shock absorbers or safety nets for the demands of life.

Personal growth was stifled as priorities were established for him and corporate values became his values. Relationships, moral choices and wellness choices that were his alone to make weren't included in the game plan. Being young, naïve and very flattered by this attention from a major corporation, he willingly sold his soul for the promise of "making it."

Now that the stakes were higher, he found that he had to work at being impressive where previously, it happened without effort. At each step of the corporate ladder, he gave away pieces of himself until the Michael we knew and loved disappeared and was replaced by a corporate clone who

101

rarely smiled. His once spontaneous sense of humor regressed into a biting cynicism. The way he spoke, the way he thought and even what he wore was carefully programmed to meet company standards. Friends were chosen on a selective basis and only if they met certain criteria. This elitism and pretentiousness cost him more than he realized.

Maintaining his corporate posture was stressful and consuming, leaving little time or energy for a home life and family. Martinis and cigarettes went a long way toward filling that void. In retrospect, he was too smart a person to be unaware that something was wrong with this picture. Nagging doubts made him uncomfortable in his own skin, though no one guessed the extent of his inner turmoil.

It was hard to penetrate the chilly exterior of his all business, no B.S. demeanor. He purposely kept people at a distance. That way, no one would find out that perception wasn't reality. From a distance, he could still be impressive and could impress because he was Michael!

In his 50s, Michael opted for an early retirement, the famous "golden handshake." Though he was rehired as a freelance consultant, the absence of corporate identity and structure proved to be the pin in his balloon of pretense. After years of ignoring serious warnings about smoking, the state of his health was critical and oxygen became a daily requirement. This coupled with long suppressed demons and insecurities completely undermined his stamina and crippled his confidence in a short period of time. Despair and uncertainty replaced his former drive and determination. Getting through each day became a painful process both physically and mentally as he sank deeper into a depression. His incredible ride was derailing and he didn't have the energy to reverse it.

As the Irish would say, the "demon drink" took over his persona and he slipped into an alcoholic freefall, hoping to drown the pain and the fears. As his life unraveled, he entered a world where operating under the influence and impaired driving accidents were frequent occurrences. The highest highs of his life were replaced with the lowest lows and degradation. He evolved from the all-American poster boy to a spent shell of his former self.

Dark days and darker moods took their toll. There was damage done and people hurt, most of all, family. His wife and sons became alienated from him and friends were few and far between. He began to phone siblings more often, as if he was looking for strength by reaching back to his roots, but never divulged too much information. We, his family, were puzzled. Though he had been both neglectful and aloof at times, we were still caught up in his past glory and reassured ourselves that he would always land on his feet and impress again—after all, he was Michael!

We were stunned when word of his sudden death arrived. Grief was surpassed only by frustration. This wasn't the right time or the right age or the right way. How could it be over so soon? Longevity runs in the family. Many lived into their 90s including his parents. What none of us realized was that his spirit had died long before his body expired. His final trip home was via UPS when the urn containing his ashes was sent home for burial in the family plot.

What a terribly sad wake-up call on how fragile and unpredictable life is, even when one seems invincible, and the importance of the old adage, "to thine own self be true." Like a shooting star, Michael's time was brief. He streaked through our lives, lit up everything around us then disappeared—breaking into pieces on the way down.

We're left with our memories, a lot of regrets and our prayers, which are ongoing…

Please God, on that final day when all are judged, have mercy on our brother, our friend, who shared our life and our time. Grant to this son of Hungry Hill, citizen of the world, successful corporate player, frightened inner child and lost soul, the peace that eluded him in his adult life.

Let there be a heaven for him and let it be what heaven was in his idyllic childhood; riding a bike, scaling stones across a mud puddle, making pea shooters in the summer and snowballs in the winter—a place where anything is possible because dreams and imagination are the only things that count. When he comes before you in that unknown arena, please forgive the negatives of his imperfect life. Please be impressed and please remember, his name was Michael!

Epilogue to Michael: I'm so glad we shared that brief window in time called childhood. All of us were drawn to your light, like moths to a flame. There's an Irish song written by Tommy Makem that proclaims, "Merry hearted boys make the best of old men." I believe with all my heart that if you had stayed true to yourself and your roots, you would have been living proof of that statement. I'm so deeply saddened that you're not.

APPENDIX A: UNSUNG HEROES

APPENDIX A

UNSUNG HEROES

In recognition of people who, through the years, did their jobs with empathy and compassion and made a difference in the lives of so many Hungry Hill (HH) residents.

Public servants – *always accessible to the needs of their HH constituents*

> Congressman Eddie Boland
> District Attorney Matty Ryan
> Judge Dan Keyes
> State Rep. Harold "Hooper" Walsh
> State Rep. Arthur McKenna
> Mayor Danny Brunton
> Mayor Tom O'Connor
> Mayor Bill Sullivan

Doctors – *conveniently located in their HH homes at all hours*

> Doctors Haggerty, Conway, Greaney, Blackmer

Hungry Hill businessmen – *credit and compassion for HH neighbors*

> Peter Hogan, T.P. Sampson, Jack & Dave Goldberg,
> Peter Loughran, Louie Zointz, James Wynne,
> Pat Leahy, Vezina's Drug Store

Hungry Hill educators – *dedicated to HH young people for decades*

Principals
Miss Abby, Miss Wilson, Miss Sheehan,
Mr. Whelan

APPENDIX A

Teachers
Our Lady of Hope School – Sisters of St. Joseph
Liberty School – Misses McMahon, Derby, Dougan,
Elliot, West, Rhodes, Smith, Kaplan
Van Sickle – Messer Golash, Kodis, Collamore,
Miss Gritzmacher

Hungry Hill musicians – *an integral part of HH social life*

John Donnellan, Jack Fitzgerald, Harold Meara,
Chris Tabb, Donnie McCarthy, The Dustmen

Our Lady of Hope Clergy – *HH spiritual needs, counseling
and comfort*
Fathers Cruse, Sexton, Power, Nickelson,
Price, Fleming

Note: These names were compiled "word of mouth" from
relatives and friends and my own personal experience.
Please know there may have been others that I forgot or
never heard about who are included in spirit.

APPENDIX B:
HUNGRY HILL NICKNAMES

HUNGRY HILL NICKNAMES

Nickname -- *a substitute name given to someone or something, usually descriptive, given in fun, affection or derision (Webster's New World Dictionary).*

Hungry Hill (HH) was a place where nicknames seemed to be in the air, part of the landscape. The following list of nicknames was compiled by the late Tom Brown, Jr. These were HH people known to him during his time on Stockman and Clantoy Streets. This list was submitted by his daughter, Marilynn Dulude.

Beppo Devine	Skipper James
Bibbers Dalton	Wimp Sullivan
Heavy Legs Garvey	Fat Foley
Bluey Bessone	Spot McDonnell
Lado Haggerty	Bunty Hoar
Cowboy Haggerty	Pee Wee Moore
Hawk Zisk	Tank Murphy
Kryl Bryda	Moose Kennedy
Beep Bryda	Jaymo Murphy
Huck Kane	Butch O'Connor
Banjo Eyes Keough	Butch Biglin
and his son,	Big Unk O'Connor
Jug Head Keough	Little Unk O'Connor
Clinkers Kennedy	Scar Bowler
Mustard Kennedy	Tossie Shea
Snake Johnson	Giggie Bryda
Pots Long	Jelly Donuts Foley
Baldy Kennedy	
Mouse Manning	
Ox McCarthy	

APPENDIX B

Through my formative years on Hungry Hill, I heard many other nicknames in passing. Some of them were known to me personally, others were submitted by Christine Lynch Keaney.

Red Garvey
Willum Garvey
Ace Manning
Fuzzy Coughlin
Muck McGovern
Wimpy Lynch
Archie Lynch
Gamo Welch
Nooner Montesi
Perry Pop
Boogie Bentley
Snots O'Connor
Honky Sawyer
Yacko Dowd
Fly Shit Dowd
BeBop Walsh
Gaf Gaffney

Fod O"Donnell
Ripper Valenti
Fritzy Crogan
Tip O'Neal
Rosco Russell
Moon Russell
Gamo Russell
Mel Roncalli
Kid Calloo
Junkie O'Connell
Red O'Shaunessey
Mickey McMahon
Blinky Carney
'B' Maloney
Moose McCarthy
Ty Tyberski

GLOSSARY

GLOSSARY

GLOSSARY OF IRISH-FLAVORED ENGLISH

I grew up in a family that included a generation of Irish immigrants. Though my grandfather and numerous great aunts and uncles only spoke English, theirs was an English with its own unique syntax and grammar. It was sprinkled with idioms and expressions known only to God and the Irish!

The following were prevalent in everyday conversation among my relatives:

haitch	The letter H
ye	You or all of you
let ye	Will you or won't you
whoosh, let ye	Will you be quiet
sit yeeze	Sit down
tis	It is
cam	Calm
amadon	Idiot, fool
affinity	A love interest
fillum	Film, movie
greenhorn	A recent Irish comeover
grand	Great or wonderful
himself/herself	He or she
after	Past tense – he is after going out (translated, he has gone out)
longheaded	Sensible, down to earth

GLOSSARY

the like of	Like, a comparison
lace curtain Irish	Historically, Irish with enough money to buy lace curtains to peek out of or Irish with fruit on the table
Shanty Irish	Irish without a "pot to pee in or a window to throw it out of," according to my relatives
God willing!	Added before or after a statement, translation: unless something happens
Tell it to Sweeney	I don't believe it
Fine broth of a man	Good looking, well-built man
Not worth a tinker's dam	Worthless, good for nothing
Looks don't boil the pot	Looks aren't important
Glory be to God or Mother of God	Exasperated
Jesus, Mary & Joseph and my Aunt's people!	Really exasperated
The Lord have mercy on his/her soul	Always added after a deceased person's name is mentioned
Little Christmas	January 6 (The Epiphany) or Three Kings Day
The Angelus*	Saying a Hail Mary three times a day

GLOSSARY

There are numerous other words and phrases that I've forgotten. Some of the above have survived three generations in my family. They were present in the speech patterns of my grandfather and my mother and her siblings and, on occasion, I find myself blurting out "mother of God" when nothing else seems to fit. God willing, a few of these sayings and traditions might survive another generation.

Ringing the angelus bells was once a daily ritual at Our Lady of Hope Church.

AFTERWORD

JOIN US FOR AN
IRISH FAMILY REUNION

CABEY, CARNEY, DILLON, DONNELLAN, LYNCH

SEPTEMBER 19-20, 2008

AT THE CLARE INN HOTEL
DROMOLAND
COUNTY CLARE, IRELAND

PLANNED ACTIVITIES:

FRIDAY, SEPTEMBER 19, 2008

•BUNRATTY FOLK PARK 10:30am -5pm The Folk Park features farmhouses, a village street, and other glimpses of historic Ireland. Then tour historic Bunratty Castle, built in 1425. Price range (includes both the park and the castle) approximately: $15-20, (a group of 20 or more and the better price).

•BUNRATTY CASTLE MEDIEVAL BANQUET 5:30 pm Built in 1425, Bunratty Castle provides a unique atmosphere for diners. Sit on long oak tables and dine by candlelight. Entertainment includes the Bunratty Singers to compliment a four course dinner with wine, all part of an unforgettable evening. Approximately: $71-$75 per person. (Again, a group of 20 or more and the better the price.)

SATURDAY, SEPTEMBER 20, 2008

•SHORT TOUR OF COUNTY CLARE 9am-5:30pm price to be determined by number of people.

•FAMILY REUNION RECEPTION AND BANQUET 7PM PRICE: $75 PER PERSON includes a buffet of four main entree choices with accompanying vegetables and salads, Tea, coffee and dessert, a bottle of wine at each table and a small donation to the Kilmaley Church in memory of our ancestors.

CÉAD MÍLE FÁILTE
(A HUNDRED THOUSAND WELCOMES)
More Than Just Words in Kilmaley

In September 2008, a reunion of the Cabey, Donnellan, Carney, Dillon and Lynch families was held at the Clare Inn just outside of Shannon Airport. Close to 100 people attended with 25 from the U.S. My grandfather and many of his siblings emigrated from Kilmaley, County Clare, Ireland, in the early 1900s and settled on Hungry Hill in Springfield, Massachusetts, a then—and now—Irish enclave.

By Thursday, September 18, just about everyone from the states had arrived at the Clare Inn. Patricia Cabey Reardon, the chief coordinator of this event had activities planned for the next few days with the reunion dinner to be held on Saturday evening, September 20. Mary Wylde, Alice Kelleher, Mary Moroney and Nuala Cabey, all from County Clare, helped her to make this a huge success. For those of us who had traveled to Ireland before, it was an opportunity to renew acquaintances with our relatives and a new experience for the first-time travelers. We were familiar with some of the Irish cousins who had attended previous reunions held in America.

Patricia had arranged for Michael O'Sullivan, who drives a mid-sized bus, to bring us around the area for a few days prior to the reunion dinner. Michael had his bus waiting promptly each morning for the next few days. Mary Fitzgerald, who once lived in Springfield, served as our tour guide as we visited places like the Burren with the portal tomb, the Cliffs of Moher, the Town of Lisdoonvarna where the world famous matchmaking festival was in full swing, the town of Doolin where we had lunch at McGann's Pub, Knappogue Castle where we experienced a medieval banquet complete

125

with entertainment between courses and a complimentary glass of mead, which tasted pretty good!

Two from our group were tapped to take part in a procession of lords and ladies at Knappogue. My nephew Chris Morris from St. Louis, Missouri, and his cousin, Jessica Morris from Feeding Hills, Massachusetts, were the Lord and Lady of Ulster. They sat at the head table with the other lords and ladies complete with crowns and robes, which made for some priceless photos!

Michael also made stops at the home of some of our relatives. We visited our ancestral home where our grandfathers were born and raised. The road up to the house in Cahermore, Kilmaley, had American flags and balloons as well as signs welcoming us to the home of our ancestors. Susan Cabey and her children had prepared a huge table outside for tea, scones, soda bread and numerous other treats. We were truly touched by their hospitality and fascinated with the fairy fort in the back of the house.

We made a stop at the Kilmaley Cemetery and viewed the graves of our ancestors, as well as the ruins of the old church. We also saw the remains of the old Kilmaley Forge, where my grandfather learned his trade as a blacksmith. Seeing and photographing Cabey's Lane in Ennis was one of the highlights of the tour for the Cabey descendants. We then stopped at the home of Kitty Cabey Quinn and her daughter, Mary Wylde, in Ennis for tea and an abundance of food and craic. Again, we were warmly welcomed by Kitty, Mary, her husband Jim and her children. The weather cooperated and we gathered outside for photos.

The big event was the reunion dinner on Saturday night, where close to 100 people gathered in the banquet hall at the Clare Inn. Mark Morris and Oliver Cabey shared emcee duties, one from each side of the Atlantic. There was a PowerPoint presentation showing pictures and facts dating back to our great grandparents.

Part of the evening's entertainment was a local storyteller, though we were hoping that some of our cousins would relate their own stories. I sat with longtime family friends, Mike and Mary Fitzgerald, and shared a few stories about the Cabey immigrants which I have compiled into a book. We were entertained by Tom Cabey and his sister, Kathy Cabey Soto. They are Cabey grandchildren and locally known musicians in the Springfield area. Many of the attendees stayed until the wee hours and sang Irish songs which we have on film.

On Sunday morning, some of us opted to attend mass at the Kilmaley Church where our forefathers worshiped, St. John the Baptist. Father McLoughlin, the Pastor, acknowledged the family reunion from the altar and welcomed us, noting that we brought good weather with us. As I sat in Church, I looked up at the open beams and tried to imagine the church in the early days when it had a mud floor, according to Fr. McLoughlin.

After mass, Johnny McCarthy of Shean, a relative of our grandmother, Aggie Frawley, waited around to meet us. We stopped at Mary Fitzgerald's home after church, presumably for tea and scones. We were surprised to walk into a lamb dinner with all the trimmings!

On Sunday afternoon, several of our group decided to walk through the woods in back of the Clare Inn and attend high tea at Dromoland Castle. Later, we gathered at Poachers Pub at the Inn to reminisce on our final evening together.

AFTERWORD

Just being in the place where my grandparents grew up and became the people they were was very enlightening. Getting to know cousins that I never knew existed and spending time with the ones I know but never see was great, or as the Irish say, it was grand! I've come to the conclusion that whoever originated the Irish saying, "Céad Míle Fáilte" must have been from Kilmaley or at least from County Clare. The royal welcome, wherever we went, was both overwhelming and gratifying. Thank you Kilmaley and County Clare for having a heart big enough for all of us. As a family we are truly blessed!

Made in the USA
Charleston, SC
05 January 2013